The PROMISE of CHRISTMAS

Joanna Kimbrel

www.thedailygraceco.com

STUDY CONTRIBUTORS

....

Illustrator:
KATIE LINSTRUM

Editor:
JANA WHITE

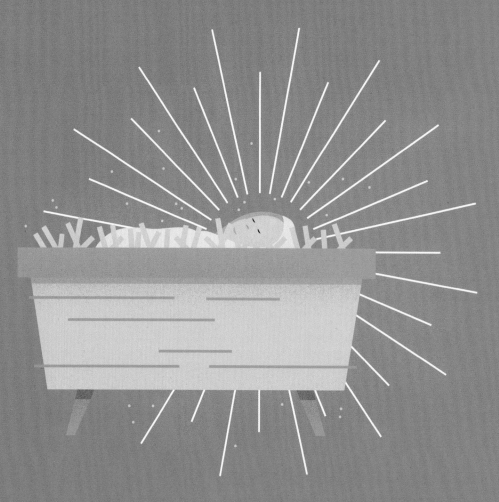

ON THE VERY FIRST
CHRISTMAS A BABY
WAS BORN IN A LITTLE
OLD BARN, WRAPPED
IN CLOTHES OLD
AND WORN.

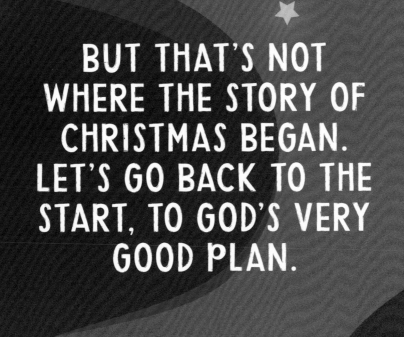

BUT THAT'S NOT
WHERE THE STORY OF
CHRISTMAS BEGAN.
LET'S GO BACK TO THE
START, TO GOD'S VERY
GOOD PLAN.

BEFORE THERE WERE
FLOWERS OR SNOWFLAKES
OR TREES, BEFORE PUPPIES
BARKED, BEFORE FISH
FILLED THE SEAS,

GOD MADE A PLAN
FROM THE LOVE
IN HIS HEART
TO MAKE PEOPLE
HIS CHILDREN,
RIGHT FROM
THE START.

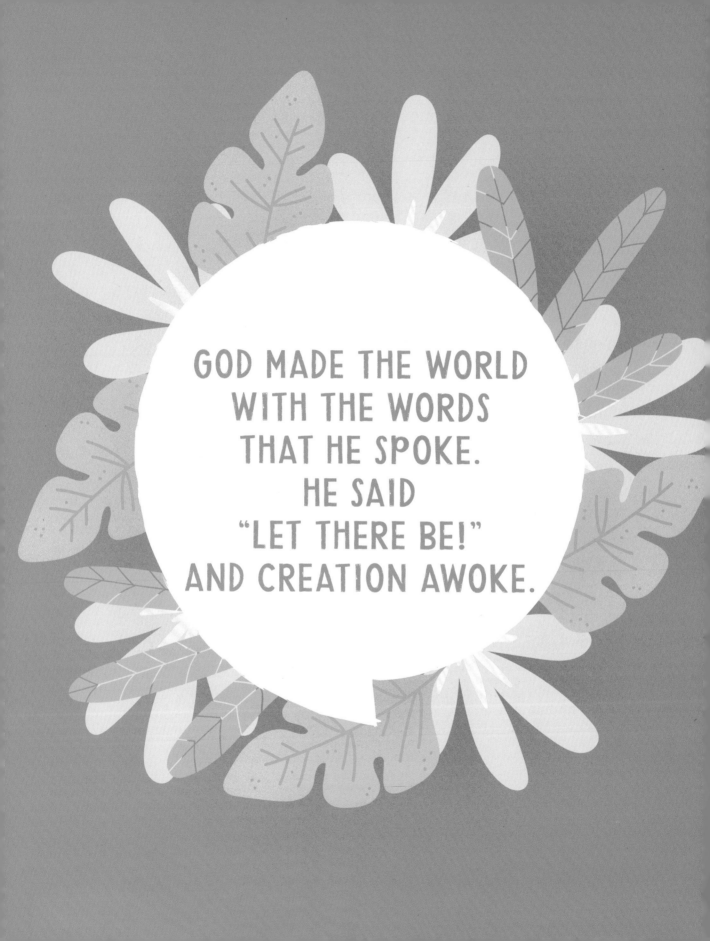

GOD MADE THE WORLD
WITH THE WORDS
THAT HE SPOKE.
HE SAID
"LET THERE BE!"
AND CREATION AWOKE.

BUT THE BEST THING HE MADE,
HE SAVED FOR THE END.
HE MADE PEOPLE, LIKE US,
AND LIVED RIGHT THERE
WITH THEM.

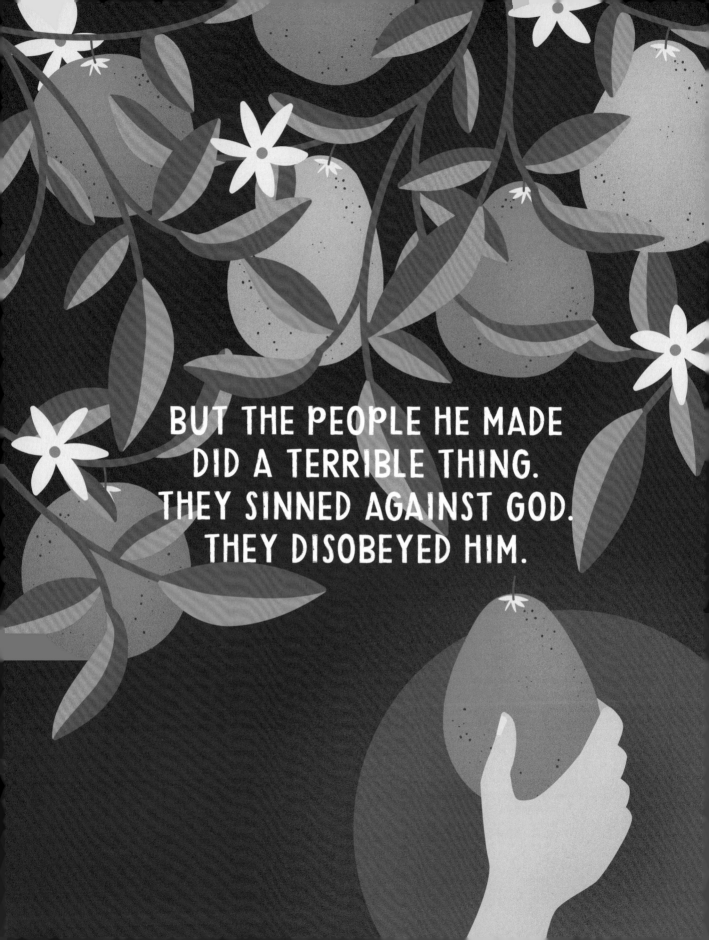

BUT THE PEOPLE HE MADE
DID A TERRIBLE THING.
THEY SINNED AGAINST GOD.
THEY DISOBEYED HIM.

HE HAD WARNED
THEM THAT SIN WOULD
CAUSE THEM TO DIE,
AND GOD SENT
THEM AWAY
WITH A TEAR
IN HIS EYE.

NOW EVERY LAST PERSON,
EACH GROWN UP AND KID,
ALL SIN AGAINST GOD,
LIKE ADAM AND EVE DID.

THAT'S WHY WE NEED CHRISTMAS,
NOT FOR PRESENTS OR LIGHTS.
GOD GAVE US CHRISTMAS TO
GIVE US NEW LIFE!

WHEN ADAM AND EVE
DISOBEYED GOD'S COMMAND
HE MADE THEM A PROMISE,
PLANNED BEFORE TIME BEGAN.

HE WOULD SEND A SMALL
BABY, HIS VERY OWN SON,
WHO WOULD SAVE US FROM ALL
OF THE EVIL WE'VE DONE.

FOR YEARS
PEOPLE WAITED
WHILE DARKNESS
CLOSED IN
FOR THE CHILD
GOD PROMISED
WOULD SAVE THEM
FROM SIN.

THEY HOPED
AND THEY
WAITED, BUT
YEAR AFTER YEAR
NO SAVIOR
APPEARED.
WAS GOD
EVEN THERE?

THE PROMISE
OF CHRISTMAS
FELT SO FAR AWAY.
THEIR HEARTS
WERE SO SICK
AND THEY LONGED
FOR THE DAY

WHEN THE FATHER
WOULD PROVE
HIMSELF FAITHFUL
TO BRING
THE CHILD WHO'D
BE THE TRUE
PROPHET, PRIEST,
AND KING.

GOD NEVER
STOPPED ACTING
TO WORK
OUT HIS PLAN
TO MAKE US HIS
CHILDREN AND LIVE
WITH US AGAIN.

THOUGH IT FELT
LIKE FOREVER,
WHEN THE TIME
WAS JUST RIGHT,
LIGHT SHONE IN
THE DARKNESS,
JOYFUL AND
BRIGHT!

AN ANGEL TOLD MARY AND
JOSEPH ONE DAY THAT
SHE'D HAVE THE BABY
WHO'D WASH SINS AWAY.

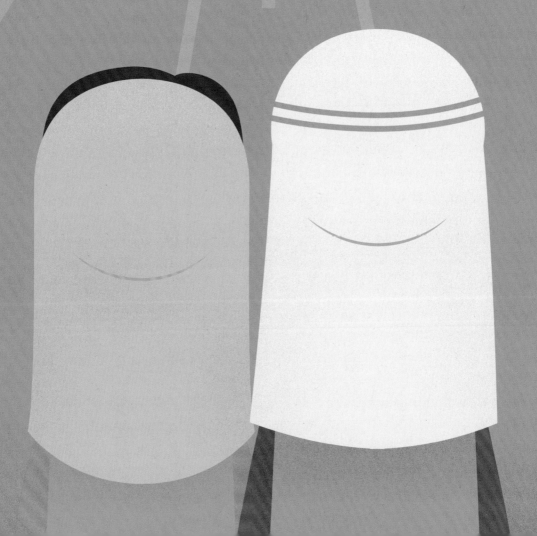

HER BELLY GOT BIGGER
UNTIL THE TIME CAME FOR
THE BIRTH OF THE BABY
WHO'D BEAR SIN AND SHAME.

THE INNS WERE ALL FULL,
THERE WAS NOWHERE TO STAY,
SO THAT BABY WAS BORN IN
A BARN ON SOME HAY.

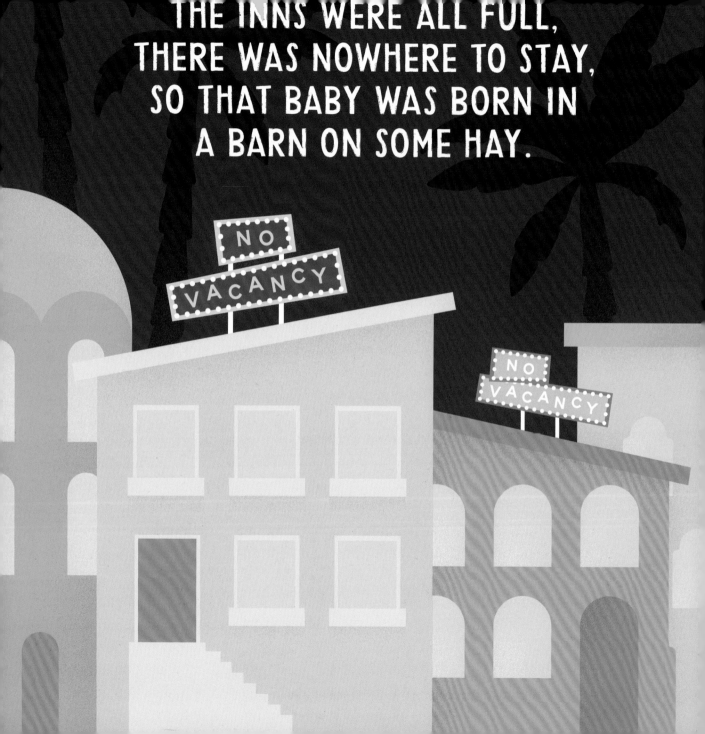

NO
VACANCY

NO
VACANCY

THEY CALLED HIS NAME JESUS,
JUST AS GOD SAID.
THE BOY WAS GOD WITH US,
GIVING LIFE TO THE DEAD.

THERE WASN'T A CASTLE,
A CROWN, OR A THRONE.
TO MANY THE BIRTH OF THE
BOY WAS UNKNOWN.

HE SEEMED PRETTY NORMAL,
BUT ANGELS DID SING
THAT THIS LITTLE CHILD WAS
THE TRUE KING OF KINGS.

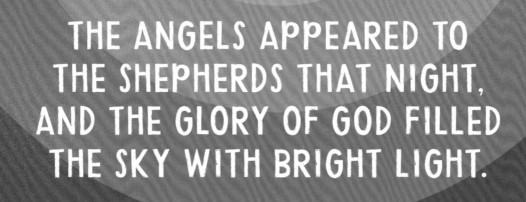

THE ANGELS APPEARED TO
THE SHEPHERDS THAT NIGHT,
AND THE GLORY OF GOD FILLED
THE SKY WITH BRIGHT LIGHT.

THE SHEPHERDS WERE SCARED,
BUT THE ANGELS PROCLAIMED:
"DON'T BE AFRAID, WE HAVE
GOOD NEWS TODAY!"

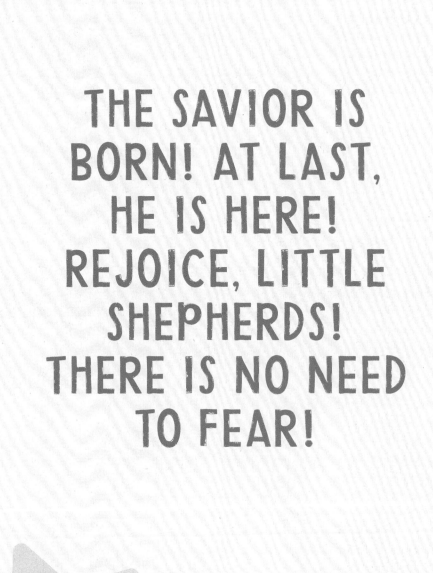

THE SAVIOR IS
BORN! AT LAST,
HE IS HERE!
REJOICE, LITTLE
SHEPHERDS!
THERE IS NO NEED
TO FEAR!

THE BABY
GOD PROMISED
TO ADAM AND EVE,
HE HAS COME!
AND HE'S BRINGING
US GREAT JOY
AND PEACE!

AND HE WOULD GROW UP,
LIKE YOU AND LIKE ME,
HE'D HAVE STINKY DIAPERS,
HE'D GET SCRAPES ON HIS KNEE.

HE'D FEEL HAPPY AND SAD
AND HAVE BELLY ACHES TOO.
HE WAS GOD HIMSELF, BUT
HE BECAME LIKE YOU.

THAT BOY
NEVER SINNED.
HE ALWAYS OBEYED.
THROUGH ALL
OF HIS LIFE
HE WAS PERFECT,
UNSTAINED.

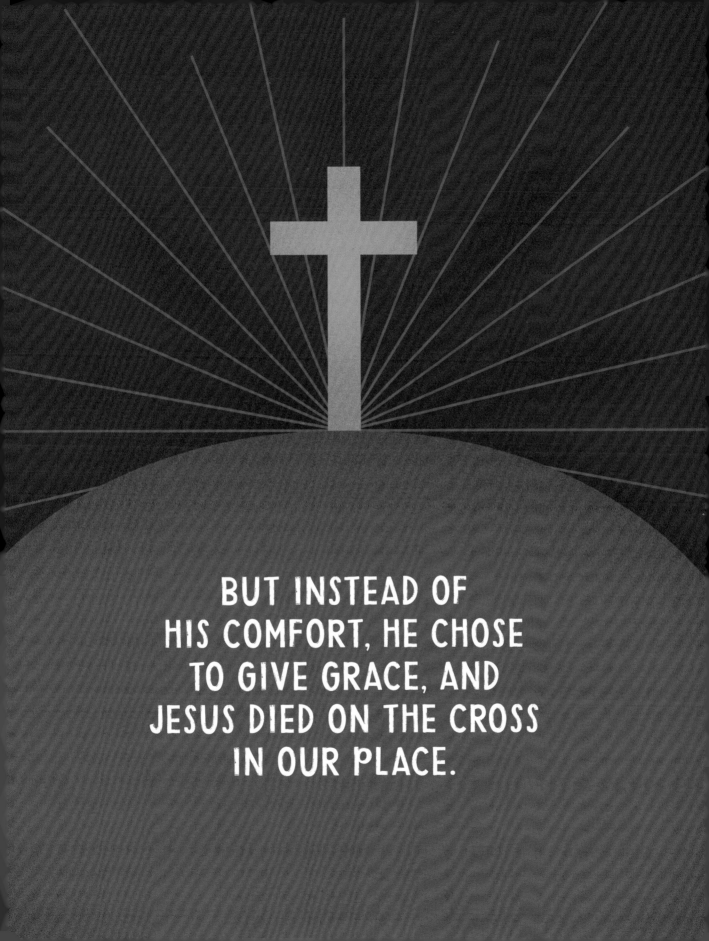

BUT INSTEAD OF
HIS COMFORT, HE CHOSE
TO GIVE GRACE, AND
JESUS DIED ON THE CROSS
IN OUR PLACE.

ON THE DAY
JESUS DIED,
HE ACCOMPLISHED
GOD'S PLAN.
THE ONE THAT
HE MADE
LONG BEFORE
TIME BEGAN.

HE PAID FOR OUR SINS,
HIS DEATH PAID THE PRICE,
BUT THEN THREE DAYS LATER,
GOD RAISED HIM TO LIFE!

AND WE CAN LIVE TOO,
IF WE TRUST NOW IN HIM,
THE ONE WHO GOD PROMISED
WOULD SAVE US FROM SIN.

HE CAME TO US ONCE, ON THAT
FIRST CHRISTMAS NIGHT,
AND HE'S COMING AGAIN
TO MAKE ALL THINGS RIGHT.

SO CHRISTMAS IS MORE THAN
A BOY IN THE HAY.
CHRISTMAS IS BETTER THAN
JUST A FUN DAY!

ON CHRISTMAS WE CELEBRATE
VERY GOOD NEWS THAT
GOD MADE A PROMISE, AND
THAT PROMISE CAME TRUE.

Thank You
for studying God's
Word with us!

CONNECT WITH US
@THEDAILYGRACECO @KRISTINSCHMUCKER

CONTACT US
INFO@THEDAILYGRACECO.COM

SHARE
#THEDAILYGRACECO #LAMPANDLIGHT

VISIT US ONLINE
THEDAILYGRACECO.COM

See you next time!